Sunwyse

Celebrating
the Sacred Wheel of the Year
in Australia

Roxanne T. Bodsworth

First published 1999
Revised edition by Hihorse Publications 2003
Revised edition by Sunwyse Writing & Celebrancy Services 2020

© Roxanne T. Bodsworth 1999

No part of this publication may be copied by any means without prior written approval of the copyright holder.

ISBN 978-0-909497-23-1

Any queries can be addressed to:
Roxanne T. Bodsworth
c/- Post Office
Eldorado VIC 3746
rbodsworth@outlook.com
sunwyse.com.au

Cover Illustration:
Steve Jolley, Jolley Enlightening

Design & Artwork:
Kathy Allen, Purple Possum Design
purplepossumdesign.com.au

Aboriginal means from the beginning
from the beginning and to the end of time
this place now called Australia is Aboriginal land
I pay my respects to the Aboriginal people
who are the traditional custodians
I pay my respects to the elders
past present future
I pay my respects

Many years ago, I began to follow the eight-spoked Wheel of the Year to deepen my awareness of the seasonal shifts and changes, but was increasingly frustrated by the inadequacy of available reference material. Everything seemed to come from the Northern hemisphere and needed translating into the Australian experience – and '**Sunwyse**' was born. The writing of this book has taken me on a fascinating journey, travelling to festivals across the country, meeting vivid and free-spirited people, while becoming ever more attuned to the seasonal cycles.

In its first run, Sunwyse found its way into the lives of Australians everywhere from obscure outposts in the desert country to the middle of the teeming cities. I realised it was part of a greater movement where many others were both searching for a way to connect with the amazing energy of this land and developing a spirituality with a distinctly Australian flavour. It is an ongoing journey for me, and there is always something new to be discovered. It is an ongoing journey for all of us.

My thanks go to the many people who have assisted and supported me in this project.

Acknowledgements

Rob Adams, Pan Pacific Pagan Alliance (PPPA); Kathy Allen, Purple Possum Design; Jose Maria Artiaga, teacher of Lakota traditions; Linda Atkinson, Michelle Bear, Alana Clarke, and Dee O'Mara, patient editors and long-suffering friends; Margrit Beemster, farmer, journalist and mentor; Ginnie Brasseaux, Catholic advisor; Danny Carey, for encouragement and support; David Carlisle, Guild of the Eclectic Shaman; Gabrielle Cleary, Applegrove Coven; David Coles, Chef, Australian Antarctic Territory, 1992; Wally Cooper, Yorta Yorta elder; Bill Easley, Jewish advisor; Stewart Farrar (dec.), Janet Farrar and Gavin Bone, wonderful witchy writers; Roger Ford, FAIRA Aboriginal Corporation; Alana Garwood, Australian Institute for Aboriginal and Torres Strait Islander Studies; Steve Gibson, Astronomer, Calgary University; Goulburn Ovens Institute of TAFE; Sheila Hollingworth, writer and motivator; Phil Hogan, amateur astronomer; Martin Ison, Church of All Worlds (CAW); Steve Jolley, artist and graphic designer; Eddie Kneebone, Pangerang Elder; Sean Knight, Curch of All Worlds; Patricia Kovacic, Hihorse Publications; William Mason, astrologer; Lisa McDonald, Green Left Weekly magazine; Thomas Konieczny, Uluru-Kata Tjuta Cultural Centre; Don McLeod, pagan writer; Hyllus Munro, Macarthur Aboriginal Liaison Unit; Marcos J. Montes, Naval Research Laboratory, Washington; Suzanne O'Neil, Larrakia elder; Clive Pickering, Light of Atlantis; Eve Plant, yoga teacher; Tavananika, wise woman and teacher of Lakota traditions; Bev and Del Richardson, Pagan Ireland; Alasdair Taylor, Eolas School of Celtic Traditions; Peregrin Wildoak, PPPA and CAW; Professor Christopher L.C.E. Witcombe, Sweet Briar College, USA; Spiral Dance, for permission to use the lyrics that complete this book.

May you never thirst.

Contents

Introduction	11
Winter Solstice	17
The Quickening	27
Spring Equinox	35
The Love Festival	43
Summer Solstice	55
The Harvest Feast	65
Autumn Equinox	73
Festival Of The Dead	79
Glossary	88
Bibliography	94

Introduction

The Wheel turns... a weakening Sun spends less and less time bringing light and warmth to Earth. In Winter's darkness, beneath Earth's surface, the seed lies dormant, resting, waiting...

The Wheel turns... after the longest night of the year, the new Sun is born. The seed wakens, readying to emerge into a world again made bright...

The Wheel turns... daily the Sun-child grows stronger. Seeds push through, daffodils appear like handmaidens to the Sun, and first lambs are born. Life follows death, Spring is coming...

The Wheel turns... a multitude of flowers welcome the warmer days. Bare trees wear lacy green, soft pink and white blossom. Babies are born; animals, birds, plants. Everything is renewing...

The Wheel turns... Burgeoning life, maturing, strengthening. Fledglings leave their nests and crops make promise of the harvest to come...

The Wheel turns... Summer's strength, blistering, blazing, raising passions. Crops turn to gold...

The Wheel turns... first harvest. Life is affirmed in Earth's bounty. Sweaty bodies test their strength and vigour.

The Wheel turns... harvest, harvest's end. The Sun grows old and thoughts turn to the coming Winter. Earth's generosity is preserved, stored against the cold. Seeds, bulbs, are set below Earth's surface...

The Wheel turns... a weakening Sun spends less and less time bringing light and warmth to Earth. In Winter's darkness, beneath Earth's surface, the seed lies dormant, resting, waiting...

Introduction

As the Sun's strength grows and diminishes, the seasons roll around as though they are part of a great wheel, the turning of which affects everyone from wheat farmers to astronauts. Physically, we depend on Earth's provision for our everyday needs. On a deeper level, it is an integral part of every community that seeks a sense of continuity, every religion that grows from a close connection to the natural world.

In an era when only the most adventurous wandered from home, before technology enabled us to operate independently of Earth's cycles, the timing of festivals was calculated according to these seasonal shifts and changes. At the beginning of Summer, the Aboriginals of North East Victoria and the Upper Murray regions gathered to feast on the Bogong Moth; on the first full moon after the Spring Equinox, the Jews celebrated the Passover; just prior to Winter Solstice, the Hopi Indians initiated their young men into the mysteries of creation.

Difficult cultures give different meanings to different times but many traditions, particularly those of European origin, simply divide the wheel into eight points: two equinoxes, two solstices, and four cross-quarter points between.

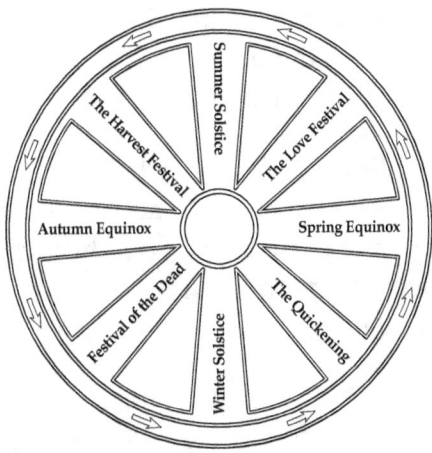

13

The Wheel provided a framework for living that gave people an affinity with the natural cycles; a connection with the rhythms of Sun and Moon and stars; and a relationship with Earth that was healthy and mutually beneficial. Routine activities like gathering food, making a fire, and preparing medicines for the sick, were sacred duties permeated with a sense of wonder.

Science, as a system of belief, displaced many of the ancient understandings, denigrating them as ignorant and superstitious. In the gaining of valuable knowledge about weather patterns, astronomy, and the ecological impact of our individual and collective behaviour, that sense of wonder has been all but lost.

Leaping over bonfires, making love in the great outdoors, or toasting to a tree's health are examples of old customs that can appear quite ridiculous in our contemporary world. Yet these practices were part of an intimate connection with Earth, and it has become imperative to reclaim that relationship if we are to achieve a sustainable existence.

For some this can be as simple as tending pot plants on a balcony; for others it means taking up the fight to preserve old-growth forests. Still others find the connection through their religious choices. For all of us, it is the building of a relationship with Earth into the pattern of our daily lives.

Since the arrival of Europeans in Australia, most of the seasonal celebrations have been calculated according to the Northern hemisphere's calendar. For more than two hundred years, we have held Winter Solstice celebrations, with hot roasts and Yule elves, in the middle of Summer.

As Australia's multicultural identity emerges, so does a distinctly Australian culture. It is drawn from Asian, African, American,

Introduction

Middle Eastern and European influences; from our history as a nation; and, not least, from the Aboriginal and Islander wisdom. Now, while drawing upon the old traditions and honouring our ancestry, we can confidently create the new.

The vastness of Australia, with its diverse seasonal patterns and geographical conditions, presents some challenges. In the Northern Territory, six seasons are recognised by the Anangu of the Uluru-Kata Tjuta National Park. At the Northern Territory's top End, the Larrakia count sixteen. In Western Australia, the Walmajarri of Fitzroy Crossing count three. The best way to gain local information is to ask the locals, and the ones who have been around the longest are the Aboriginals.

Sunwyse is intended as a starting point for those wishing to explore the Wheel of the Year as it turns in their own lives, rather than a definitive guide. Each chapter contains suggestions for celebrating but there are as many traditions as there are people. The Jewish calendar is set in Jerusalem while that of the Catholics is determined in Rome. Some Australian pagans choose to follow the Northern hemisphere dates as a way of building a world-wide unity of purpose.

Following the Wheel cannot be a static way of life. It cannot be dogmatic or unchanging. It is motion, a journey through stars and seasons, through other worlds, through our own conscious awareness and inherent wisdom. It is following the cycles of life, growth, death, and rebirth until no longer is there any separation between following the Wheel and being part of it; no longer any separation between Earth and her children.

Winter Solstice
21 June

Sunwyse

The Wheel turns... after the longest night of the year, the new Sun is born. The seed wakens, readying to emerge into a world again made bright...

The Sun hangs low over the horizon, barely seeming to move in its passage across the sky. The days are short; the nights are long. In the Southern hemisphere, the shortest day and the longest night occur between 20 and 23 June. (In the Northern hemisphere, the Winter Solstice is known as Yuletide and coincides with the Christmas celebrations.) Light snow falls on the mountains, frost lies across the valleys. A cold easterly wind, walpya mankurra, makes its way across the sunburnt West. In the Australian Antarctic Territory, the old Sun has ceased to rise at all, ceding its authority to the long night.

> *A man wrapped in rubber dives into the Antarctic sea through a hole drilled in the thick ice. Before descending deeper into the darkness in search of sea-life, he directs the narrow beam of his torch onto the stalactites formed beneath the sea's surface. Nature has been at her most skilful, crafting intricate upside down ice-castles that glitter in the light like something alive.*
>
> *In this strange place, the diver records fine details about the life that survives here, the krill and sea urchins and the lichens. As his own temperature drops lower until his muscles feel taut and painful, he wonders that anything lives in this.*
>
> *When his tasks are finished the diver emerges into the frozen wonderland. His gaze wanders to the horizon, hoping to glimpse a Sun that has deserted them. It is not to be found, has not been sighted for weeks past, and then only for a few moments. It will not be seen for weeks to come. Through chapped lips, he mutters the aching words written by another expeditioner in another year:*

Winter Solstice

*"Half the year has come and gone
and we have all but lost the Sun
and sometimes it may seem strange
that all's the same, there is no change."**

No animals cross the snow-packed land as he walks back to the base. No birds fly past. The last elephant seal lumbered away in March and will not return until November. There are only the sea-creatures beneath the frozen sea, and the other Australians who form part of this year's team.

Sometimes it seems the darkness is as much in their hearts and minds as in the landscape. But Midwinter nears, the turning-point for Earth in her journey around the Sun, the turning-point for the year they have weathered in this strange place.

Already they have sent the invitations to select celebrities. The Queen Mother has sent her apologies but they haven't yet heard from Miss Universe. The chef has been immersed in his recipe books, choosing a menu with Cocktail de homard; Basse Côte de Porc Rôtie; Sorbet; Homard Cardinal; Tournedos Bordelaise; and Profiteroles Au Chocolat; with a complimentary selection of fine wines and liqueurs.

It will be a day of crazy games culminating in a concert of extraordinary talent and a dazzling fireworks display. Though they will then have to wait another six weeks before the next sighting of the Sun, no others in the Southern hemisphere will party quite the same.

To the mainland of Australia where the old Sun still shows his face but moves slowly across the sky, hanging low over the horizon when once he marched proud and high. The freshwater crocodile lays her eggs, then carefully buries them in the river sand to keep them from harm.

* *Year Book*; Neil *'Noddy'* Cain, Diesel Mechanic, AAT Davis, 1987.

The goanna hibernates, sustained by the store of fat it has built up in the preceding months. The currawong has deserted the mountain heights for the foothills and plains.

At the house where this year's solstice celebrations will be held, a friend arrives with a great redgum log loaded in his trailer. Many hands reach to help and they lug it inside, pushing and straining, some shrieking as spiders and ants flee from beneath the disturbed bark. Two of the men exchange a wary look; there has been bitterness between them in the past months. The younger tentatively offers his hand and the older moves forward to clasp it firmly.

"Weapons aside?" he says. The younger nods eagerly.

Despite pushing and shoving and kicking, the log refuses to fit into the fireplace. One man sucks on his grazed knuckles, and suggests it fits well enough on the broad tiled hearth in front. There is careful examination to make sure the log will not set the house alight if left out of the fireplace. A compromise is reached with the log half-in, half-out. Kindling is carefully arranged around it and then the children, who have been waiting less than patiently on the sidelines, are allowed their part.

They drag forward a basket filled with evergreen plants – citrus, gum leaves, wattle – and decorate the log. The father takes a bottle of cider and pours it liberally over the wood. The mother hands him a smouldering stump saved from last Yule to be used for the lighting of this year's log. Everybody cheers as the fire splutters into life.

While the grown-ups share a well-earned cup of cider, the children begin decorating the house. Evergreen plants, brightly coloured paper lanterns, shining stars, painted ornaments, and mirrors to reflect the beauty of the candlelight. When it is done, the house has been transformed into a temple of good cheer.

Outside is deep darkness. As coloured lights are woven around an apple tree, it lifts its branches in welcome, but they slowly become weighed down with gifts of nuts and fruits and little toys for the elves – magick is needed to prepare the way for the Sun-child. Prayer-ties are added, hanging like butterflies and dancing in the breezes. When it is done, the grown-ups, bringing their cider, come to see the children's work.

Someone requests a song of blessing for the tree. Faces are blank, until another suggests that any cheerful song would be appreciated. The only song everyone knows is 'Roll out the barrel' so they give a very happy rendition of that classic.

"To the tree! Long and healthy life!" toasts one, toasts all, as they pour the remainder of their drink around the base of the tree in blessing. Bright eyes watch from the branches and bushes. When the food hung from the tree is gone the next morning, and the prayer-ties have been opened, who is to say it was not the elves.

Gifts are exchanged amidst more toasts to each other's health. Soon the floor is covered in bright-coloured wrapping paper. Singing and dancing and feasting, the revellers seem light-filled, glowing.

Not everyone has the strength to keep vigil to dawn, but some do. As the weary stayers look into the flickering flames, they begin to see shapes forming and moving within the gleaming coals. The vision grows stronger until they see clearly that it is two warriors, one wearing the mask of a bull and the other wearing a wolf's head. They are battling for the Sun, as they have done since the world was born.

In a slow dance, the warriors circle each other, weapons raised, thrust and defend, withdraw and circle again. As wolf-man falls amid the glowing embers, the new Sun reaches gently over the horizon with a soft display of gold-threaded sky.

✻ *Sunwyse*

Ways of celebrating:

✻ There are usually a few community events taking place around this time. The 'Irish Christmas' is a peculiarly Australian paradox, with feasting and dancing and Irish music. Some communities hold artist's parties with offerings of poetry and song, storytelling and drama. This expression of their creative fire-energy holds a certain attraction for the light, speeding its return. Many pagan groups hold Yuletide celebrations open to anyone.

✻ The Queen's Birthday weekend is held on the second weekend in June (except in Western Australia where it is later in the year) and is the official opening for the ski season. There is rarely enough snow to actually ski, so those who make their way to the snowfields can spend much of the weekend sipping port around an open fire in one of the taverns, swapping stories with friends and strangers. A very Midwinter way of being!

✻ The Roman midwinter once included the Saturnalia festival, a time outside of time which kept the Julian calendar accurate. It involved several days – some say twelve – given over to riotous fun, religious rites, gift-giving, public gambling, and the closure of shops, schools and law courts. All fighting was suspended, roles were reversed so that masters waited upon slaves, and misers became uncharacteristically generous. A bit of old-fashioned role reversal during Midwinter festivities always adds to the fun e.g. wearing masks, cross-dressing or theme parties.

✻ Following the shortest day of the year is Mother's night when the universe labours to birth the Sun-child. Wait upon mothers, giving them the most comfortable seats, cooking a special meal, maybe treating them to a foot massage.

Winter Solstice

- Dies Natalis Solis, the Birth of the Unconquered Sun, is a time for remembering the birth of the divine child, be that Apollo, Jesus, Osiris or Frey. Children are the ones who lead the way into the future and this is their festival. A birthday cake for the Sun is usually well-received, with each child lighting a candle and making a wish for the coming year.

- There are many fun activities associated with this festival that can help to fill in the time over the school holidays, such as making decorations like paper chains and lanterns to bring a touch of colour to the home. An old English game that symbolised the survival of the Sun involved throwing a gold or silver ball between two teams, trying to keep it in the air.

- A generous visit from the spry green-suited Yule-elf, the ancestor of the modern-day Santa Claus, need not pose any conflict with the children's understanding of the red-suited Santa Claus who comes at Summer's solstice. It may even help them to link the two turning points of the year.

- Decorating the house with plants that survive the Winter symbolises the survival of the green and can teach children (and adults) about the difference between deciduous and perennial, and the place of these plants in the Australian climate. A living tree is strung with coloured lights and gifts of fruit and nuts in the hope that the elves, feeling generous in return, will grant the unspoken wishes.

- Another family activity is to weave a wreath of wishes, made of evergreen branches with nuts and sprigs of holly for the Yule spirits. This is placed on the front door as a sign of welcome and goodwill.

- ❊ Because of the poor weather, Midwinter is a time when people are forced to remain in close proximity with each other. Weapons are laid at the door before entering the hall where a Yuletide feast is being held. It is a chance to put aside conflict, perhaps re-establishing contact with family members, making long-awaited apologies or even becoming involved in peace activism.

- ❊ For many, it is a cold and lonely time. Reaching out to those usually forgotten or disregarded can make everyone feel that little bit warmer. This is another area where the children can be involved, learning to enjoy the giving as well as the receiving.

- ❊ In European tradition, an oak stump was used for the Yuletide fires because of the wood's ability to burn for a long time while generating good heat. Australia has many such timbers that meet the same need e.g. yellowbox, river redgum, redbox. In keeping with the spirit of generosity, the Yule log should either come from the host's land or be a gift. It is decorated with evergreen plants, sprinkled with corn or wheat flour, doused with cider/ale and lit with a piece saved from last year's log. Where a hearth is lacking, a smaller log can be used and topped with three white candles, lit with last year's candle stub.

- ❊ In the Northern hemisphere, the Yule log was kept burning for the twelve days from Christmas to the Epiphany. Some choose instead to light the log each evening, or burn it only through the longest night. Whatever is chosen, the Yule log or candles represent the warmth of the hearth and must not be allowed to go out before the designated time. When it does go out is the moment to make oaths and resolutions for the coming year.

- Livestock can be blessed by mixing some of the ashes with their drinking water. Similarly, mixing some ash (which contains the nutrient potash) with the seed to be sowed for harvest charges the seed with the energy of fire.

- The wassail bowl containing spiced and warmed cider or mead is taken around the neighbours, with singing, as a way of spreading good cheer and announcing Yuletide peace. The bowl is then shared with family and friends in a night of drinking, toasting and stories that grow ever bigger and better. Trees are wassailed with singing and the remainder poured around the base as a blessing for fruitfulness.

In a physical, psychological and spiritual sense, celebrating the Winter Solstice can help us make the transition from darkness to light. As the Wheel moves forward, the new Sun grows stronger, the days ever-longer, and the world grows warmer, more welcoming.

The Quickening
31 July

 Sunwyse

The Wheel turns... daily the Sun-child grows stronger. Seeds push through, daffodils appear like handmaidens to the Sun, early Spring lambs are born. Life follows death, Spring is coming...

The festival of the Quickening, also called by the Celtic name of Imbolc, marks the end of Winter; life is stirring beneath Earth's surface like a quickening in the womb. The wattle's blossom has captured the Sun's colour and the magpies are busy swooping any who dare step within their territory. Yet, despite these signs of impending fruitfulness, the Winter stores are at their lowest.

Celebrated from sundown on 31 July to sundown the next day, the Quickening is the final feast before commencing a time of purification and fasting similar to the Lenten period preceding the Easter celebrations. (Occurring in early February in the Northern hemisphere, the Quickening is more commonly known as the Christian festival of Candlemas.) In both the Celtic and Roman Catholic traditions, this festival is dedicated to Brighid. She is the sainted Goddess of poetry, healing and smithcraft, who moves across the land softening with her white wand that which was rendered hard with Winter frosts.

> *It has been a sunny, cloudless day and the women have worked hard cleaning Winter's stagnation from the house. Windows are open to let in the crisp air, curtains float on the Hill's hoist like bridal trains; buckets of soapy water are tipped over the ground already sodden from recent rains. On the nearby plain, karnanganyja the emu can be seen out strolling with wirnini-wirnini, her brood of chicks.*
>
> *A short, plumpish woman sees a bucket with a short metal spade sitting against the fence. She goes over to investigate and finds the bucket filled with cold, crumbling clods of earth. Tied to the spade is a ribbon and a daffodil.*
>
> *She calls to the other women.*

"The dwarves have broken the ground ready for Spring."

With the house freshened, the women look to their own rituals of purification. One heads for the shower. Another works with meditation and sweet-smelling smudge sticks. A third fills the bath with lavender-scented water and lowers herself in gently. The day fades into dusk.

Robed in white, they gather in the candlelit room. Among them is a maiden being admitted to this sisterhood for the first time; her moonflow has recently begun and she is to be regarded as a woman. With the remnants of the Yuletide decorations, a woman lights the fire in the hearth.

Their hands sculpt paper on which sigils and messages have been drawn. There is a frenetic energy in the way the sculptures are tossed into the fire, voices rising high and crashing down like ocean waves as they name what it is they discard. Then, breath is slowly expelled and shoulders relax as they watch the burdens of the year past flare brilliantly and fall into clean white ash.

There is laughter now, voices easy and comfortable. Gradually, the talk fades and the candlelit room is filled with waiting, waiting...

A loud knocking. The maiden jumps like a startled deer, giggles nervously. The woman of the house steps forward to answer the door. The maiden strains to see who is there, but the visitor is cloaked and her identity hidden. Yet it seems the others know her.

"Fàilte ort a Bhride. Welcome, Brighid," says the woman of the house.

Brighid enters with her basket of rushes and lays them in the middle of the women to be later formed into her crosses. From her cloak, she draws a slim white wand topped with a clear quartz that captures the sparkling light of the candles and of the maiden's eyes. Brighid's mantle flares behind as she circles the room.

"Beannacht le na daoine an tighe seo. God bless the people of this house," she says before quietly departing.

The women form a sheath of oats into a Brideog, effigy of the maiden Brighid, representing her spirit still present. They dress her in women's clothing and, midwives now, lay her in a cradle near the hearth. Each brings their offering, thanking also the women who have been their guides and teachers over the year past. Soon, the Brideog is surrounded by flowers. A quartz crystal is placed over her heart.

The mood deepens among the women. The candles flicker. With unblinking eyes, and the fire crackling like firm footsteps through the bush, they move slowly, solemnly, carefully. One woman draws a rose crystal from her pocket and places it beside the Brideog, speaking a vow to be open and gentle of heart. She lights her candle and holds it before her as though to light the way forward into a new year.

Another offers an opal and vows to let the truth be seen, then lights the flame. The maiden is the last, placing a fragile sea-shell beside the Brideog. She speaks in a whisper.

> "I will be faithful to my self.
> I will respect my sex.
> I will honour all women."

Tears well in her eyes as she is drawn into the embrace of the others. The grandmother places a crown of candles on her head and lights them carefully. "Hail to the Spring Maiden," she says.

The maiden dances, foolishly, drawing laughter and ribaldry from the others, dancing as Brighid danced to draw the marauding soldiers' attention away from the fleeing Virgin Mary and baby Jesus.

"Hail to the Spring Maiden," call the other women. "Hail to the Spring Maiden."

Ways of celebrating:

- ❊ The promise of Spring weather brings a surge of optimism and energy; a good time for getting the garden ready for Spring planting and thoroughly cleaning the house. In Ásatrú mythology, this festival, called 'Disting' in Norse, is associated with the dwarves because of their ground-breaking skill. The wisdom of the dwarves is present whenever garden tools are used to turn over the soil in readiness for Spring planting and whenever those tools are carefully maintained.

- ❊ The recognition of Brighid at this festival is, like St. Patrick's day, a recognition of the Celtic heritage that has found its way into much of Australian culture. As she is the Goddess of poetry and fire, this feasting is a good time for poetry and storytelling around a bonfire or open fireplace.

- ❊ Brighid, or her representative, is welcomed by the woman of the household. She brings rushes or straw and gives her blessing before departing. A 'brideog', a doll-like effigy of Brighid, is made from a sheaf of the rushes, or straw, dressed in women's clothing and placed in a cradle beside the hearth as a blessing for fertility.

- ❊ A piece of unbleached linen, the 'brat Bhride' is left outside from sundown to sundown to receive Brighid's blessings and then kept in the house for the following year.

- ❊ With life stirring beneath Earth's surface like a quickening in the womb, it is very much a feminine festival and women may gather by themselves for Lá Fhéile Bríd, the feast of Brighid.

This takes many forms, depending upon those present, but one way is for each woman to light her own candle, taking responsibility for carrying the light into the new year. Vows are made for the coming time; written, spoken or otherwise represented e.g. with crystal offerings.

❈ The straw and rushes can also be woven into St. Brighid's Cross, the *Criosog Bridghe*. One is placed on the front door, inviting her presence and fertility. Any remaining rushes/straw are buried the next day and last year's crosses are burned, along with leftover Yuletide decorations, as part of the early Spring cleaning.

St. Brighid's Cross, *Criosog Bridghe*.

❈ Women who have played an important role are honoured by toasting to them, offering a prayer, or making them a gift. Such simple acknowledgment can be very much appreciated. In the yogic tradition, the full moon in July is the birthday of all gurus, a time to honour all guides and teachers with prayers, letters, gifts, public accolades or private rituals such as planting a flower.

The Quickening

- Brahma, the creator-god, is invoked at this same full moon to destroy death and bring life, with the burning of burdens from the past year and prayers for renewal. The way is then clear to make offerings for health, happiness and prosperity. One of the many ways to 'draw down the moon' is to capture its reflection in a goblet of water and then pass the cup amongst each other.

- On a lighter note, 1 August is the birthday of all horses in the Southern hemisphere. While gurus may show the way, horses have helped carry us across the generations. To the Romany, the horse was a gift from the Goddess to help the people. In many cultures, the horse is considered a sacred animal and this equine birthday is a good time to give an extra pat, an apple or a good rub-down to a friendly horse (with the owner's permission).

The Quickening brings with it the first restless movements that push us forward, beginning a journey into the light when the Sun will return in equal measure to the darkness. It is a gentle time, an awakening, a realisation that life never really stands still.

Spring Equinox
21 September

 *Sunwyse*

The Wheel turns... a multitude of flowers welcome the warmer days. Bare trees weary lacy green, soft pink and white blossom. Babies are born; animals, birds, plants. Earth is renewing...

When day and night come back into balance, people emerge from their closed-up houses and step into the world again. The snows melt on the highlands, filling the waterways. Senses are bombarded by fresh scents, bright colours and the voices of happy children. With so much wonder about, it would seem that no-one remains unaffected.

The Spring Equinox falls between 20 and 23 September and is considered the astrological New Year. Though day and night hang in balance, it is sure that light will emerge the victorious and the days will grow longer from now until the Summer Solstice. (In the Northern hemisphere, this equinox occurs in March as is celebrated as Easter.)

> *The colours and perfumes of flowers invade the senses across the continent, from the West, where the wind begins to blow hot and dry, to the East where the rainfall mingles with the melting snow.*
>
> *Persephone emerges from the Underworld and is welcomed by Demeter, Earth Mother, who causes seeds to sprout and flowers to bloom in celebration. Mother and daughter reunited, they dance through the paddocks as the world explodes into colour around them.*
>
> *Ostara, Herald of the Sun, calls all creatures to emerge from their warm burrows and hearths to greet the world renewed, to greet the SunPrince grown to maturity and ready to warm Earth to fruitfulness.*
>
> *There is a faint lightening of the over-clouded night as the mother rouses the children from their sleep. They dress quickly in the chill air*

Spring Equinox

and breakfast mostly in silence, eyes still foggy with sleep. As they pile into the car, excitement takes over and young voices are raised as they speak their plans for the day.

"I'm going on the Octopus three times at least," says one.

"I'm going to win one of those fairy princess dolls," says the girl.

"Well, don't come looking for me when all your money's spent," says the mother. "And don't spend it all on show bags before you've had a good look around."

"Will Sirius win a ribbon?" asks the youngest, speaking of the Angus bull they delivered to the grounds the day before.

The mother smiles. "Your father certainly thinks so," she says. "We'll have to wait and see."

When they reach the showgrounds, the children pile out and begin to disperse, returning reluctantly when called back to help unload the car of its crafts and produce. Once the displays are organised, the children take off at a run, terrified they might miss out on some of the sights.

Olwen, White Lady of the Day, walks before them, long golden hair streaming, anemone fingers attired in many rings, and wearing a collar of red gold. Wherever her feet have trodden, flowers bloom and the children dance in her footprints, delighted.

"She's a sure bet to win Miss Show Girl," says a watching bystander.

There is so much to see and do: the nursery with its pups and lambs and ducklings; the exotic chooks; the snake handler; the side-shows *with their noise and colour; the Aboriginal story-teller; horse-riding events; wood-chopping; shearing; and the grand parade of the finest animals.*

The clouds disperse mid-morning, chased away by fiery arrows cast by a determined bright angel. This is Spring-time and darkness has lost the battle to control the year.

As evening draws down, torch-bearers advance up the hill. They are dressed in filmy robes and bring flute and lyre, pipe and drums. They join hands, dancing sunwyse around the fire, singing and making music. The SunLord dances with the flower-crowned Spring Maiden, the wind quickening their steps as they leap higher and higher over the flames in a dance of fertility.

All is in balance, day and night, male and female, life and death. When weariness comes to the dancers and bards, it is the weariness of having battled through the cold times to reclaim the warmth. It is a good weariness.

Ways of celebrating:

❊ With the brighter days, Spring cleaning has the effect of clearing Winter's cobwebs from both the house and the mind. To take this cleansing onto a more ritualistic level, silken chords are used to represent that which has bound us during the Winter months, and breaking the chords demonstrates release.

❊ The Jewish celebration of the Ten Days of Repentance begins with Rosh Hashanah, the Jewish New Year, and extends to Yom Kippur, the Day of Atonement. The actual dates vary from year to year according to the Jewish calendar but Rosh Hashanah usually falls within the month of September or early October. As part of the ritual, clothes are thrown into the river, discarding the old life. An alternative that is nevertheless in keeping with this sentiment, can see discarded clothes donated to charitable groups or used as biodegradable weed-mats in the garden.

❊ The Aussie Rules Football Grand Final sees the Winter sports season draw to a close with a great deal of ribaldry and fanfare. For some, this means their time (and television) is freed up for other matters. Others feel bereft and must look for new ways to occupy their minds and bodies.

❊ Spring Equinox is a time for singing, music, dancing, poetry and feasting; for picnics and the sharing of sweet wine, or cakes and bread. As occurs at Easter-time, decorated eggs are exchanged as symbols of fertility. Hot cross buns represent the balanced Sun.

Sunwyse

- ❃ The annual Wiccan conference, combining workshops with a Spring Equinox ritual, is held in a different state each year. Wherever hilltop fires are lit to welcome the light, the land will bear fruit and homes will be secure as far as the fire's glow extends.

- ❃ The blossoming Earth reawakens a fierce love within us and we are reconciled with her by promises to protect and care for Earth, perhaps becoming involved in clean-up days or tree-planting weekends. With all the flowers, there are plenty to both decorate the house and adorn the body with garlands of leaves and daisy chains.

- ❃ Canberra hosts a flower festival called Floriade, and the annual round of agricultural shows begins, with displays of farm produce and husbandry, and carnival atmospheres.

- ❃ According to Greek mythology, Persephone is carried off into the Underworld by Hades at the Autumn Equinox but re-emerges to be reunited with her mother, Demeter, at the Spring Equinox. Any re-enactments of this drama tend to include a great deal of ad-libbing but the theme remains incorruptible: the renewal of relationships between mothers and daughters. This can be as simple as sharing a picnic, going to the theatre, picking a bunch of flowers, or the more involved process of reaching a hand across an emotional gulf. Where the options are limited, there are always letters that can be written and symbolically burnt or buried. Perhaps even lighting a candle and uttering a prayer of reconciliation.

- ❃ Buddhists teach that when day and night are in balance, Buddha comes to Earth for a week and leads stray souls to

Nirvana. The Japanese* visit cemeteries with food and sake, offering incense, flowers and prayer for their dead. While this may sound somewhat sombre, it is regarded as a festive occasion.

Spring Equinox is a time of transition from darkness to light, of balancing between the two just for a moment to grasp our bearings and make sure we are facing the right direction. It is a time of heightened senses and reaching out for the promise of things to come.

---

* This festival occurs during March in Japan.

The Love Festival
31 October

The Wheel turns... burgeoning life, maturing, strengthening. Fledglings leave their nests and crops make promise of the harvest to come...

The breezes lose the last of their Winter chill and instead become soft, balmy. The Bogong Moths have begun their long migration from the sunny climes of Queensland towards the high plains of Victoria, stopping over in Sydney on the way and causing much concern with blocked vents and pipes. Ducks line the waterways with their broods, and fledgling magpies with their soft, grey plumage are learning to fly. Baby freshwater crocodiles break through their shells and crawl out of the sand into a frighteningly vivid and dangerous world. Celebrated in the Northern hemisphere as Mayday and often called Beltane, the Love Festival heralds the beginning of Summer.

> *All the fires, every candle and every hearth, are extinguished as night falls. The druid climbs the hills above the township to where the wood has been laid for the Bel-fire. He calls upon the power of the Sun to come and warm Earth, help the crops grow and the fruit to ripen. The wood slowly starts to smoulder under the friction of the bow-drill. It glows dull red and, suddenly, bursts into flame.*
>
> *Revellers, who will help keep the fire burning throughout the night, begin to arrive. The young men and women drift off among the trees, to collect nuts and fruit and boughs to decorate their homes. Beneath a canopy of ghost gums and stars, they embrace and discover loving, awakening the fertility of Earth through their own bodies.*
>
> *In the shadows stands a handsome stag, Cernunnos, the Horned One. In sudden joy he rears and races through the trees, leaping the creek and dashing down the hillside. His consort waits in a paddock with the green wheat reaching, yearning, for the Sun's warmth. She weaves her arms around him, weaves youthful dreams and rainbow*

promises around him. They lie together in the hieros gamos, the sacred marriage, blessing the harvest with their love.

When the Sun rises, each of the townsfolk takes a glowing stick from the diminished fire and carries it to their home, there to rekindle the warmth of their hearth. The greenwood lovers drift back slowly, with sleepy eyes and tousled hair. On the way down the hill they laugh, speaking of the faerie folk encountered during the night.

A crone, in shimmering green, calls the children and stands behind them as they knock on doors. The householders answer with their gifts and the children's baskets brim over with flowers, fruit, and sweet biscuits. As they leave each house, the green woman raises her hand and draws a sigil of blessing, for prosperity.

The townsfolk gather around the ancient tree, Earth's oldest lover, with strong roots reaching deep into her womb. They attach ribbons, all the colours of the rainbow, to a hawthorn hoop. There are some red, for healing, some green, for fertility, and blue for wisdom.

A tall man throws the hoop high into the trees, the ribbons trailing behind like a tail of silken fire. He misses and the hoop comes tumbling down again, to much laughter. Good-natured, he grins and tries again, and again, and again until it loops over a branch. When it does not fall to his sharp tug, the townsfolk cheer.

With a soft smile at her greenwood lover, a young woman in full-skirted costume walks forward and chooses a green ribbon. He hesitates, then joins her and chooses one that is blue. Others join in and the drumming begins. They dance around the tree, weaving over, under, over each other, chanting:

"We are the flow, we are the ebb,
  We are the weavers, we are the web."

Others join in, darting in quickly and seizing a ribbon. The pace builds, faster and faster until they become a whirling rainbow around the tree. With a final ecstatic cry, the drums stop and the dancers fall to the ground, panting and content.

The tree, in its rainbow garment of wishes and dreams, watches over them like a benevolent father. Slowly the dancers lift themselves from the ground and go to join the feasting.

As the full moon rises and the heavy, tangible scent of roses and jasmine fills the air, women take the brooms from the closet. What seemed a mere tool of domestic felicity is transformed into a vehicle of freedom, carrying them to sacred gatherings in parks and city centres across the world.

Some are dressed in soft, flimsy dresses with their hair unbound. Some in bright, crazy attire like carnival costumes. Others wear faded jeans and T-shirts with political slogans: "Breaking the Silence", "Reclaim the Night", "No more violence". All are dressed as they please.

When greetings have been exchanged, the crone recalls them to their purpose and the chants begin. As their voices grow stronger, louder, so do their hearts and they move out, eagerly, onto the streets. They have summoned a wild wind, and it sweeps through the plum trees lining the roads, stripping them of blossoms and scattering them over the path.

Drivers beep their horns and people hang over the balconies, calling out. The calls are lost among the echoing sounds of women, in every country, reclaiming the night; the chanting voices, the drum-beats, the thousands of feet striking the streets with purpose. The women are *unsure if calls from the watchers have been in support or contempt, but they keep marching.*

When they reach the riverbank, they set the bonfire alight, dancing and singing as the flames rise up. Some of these women are healers, seers, midwives, and remember a time when they would have been consigned to the hungry flames. Like the phoenix, they have risen again and claim the fire, the element of power and purification, for their own.

As they sink onto the ground and rest by the fire's warmth, one woman shares a story of the time when she was jailed for breast-feeding her baby on a bus. Another has left the violence of her marriage and tells of her struggle to create a new life for her family. There is a teenage girl who, raped by a family friend, prepares to relive the ordeal and be judged by a panel of twelve strangers.

The crone rises and pulls the girl to her feet. She takes three sticks from the fire and teaches the girl to fire-dance, tossing the sticks into the air, catching them and whirling. The girl discovers she has a talent for the craft.

Laughter and tears, belly-dancing and song, story-telling and wise listening, all weave on through the night. In this place is safety, love, and healing wisdom. It is a hard place to leave, but as the night ends the women return their broomsticks to the closet and close the door. Yet they treasure the vision given them by the crone and know themselves transformed.

"One day," the crone pronounced, "our daughters will know a world without sexual violence, a world where women are honoured and their moonflow held sacred. We march because we believe such a world is possible. We march to create such a world."

� *Sunwyse*

Ways of celebrating:

✤ The Bel-fire, commemorating a Celtic god of light, is made with friction by using a bow drill. It is the summoning of the Sun's energy to fire the wood from which all other fires are kindled from now until Samhain, the Festival of the Dead. The fire is kept burning all through the night and, in the morning, each person takes a still-glowing stick, called the fire-seed, to light their hearths.

✤ While in many areas the end of October is an ideal time for bonfires, with the warm days and cool nights, some areas of Australia are already well on their way to Summer dryness. It is important to check with local authorities before attempting a Bel-fire on a hill-top. The sound of approaching fire sirens would not add to the ambience of the festival.

✤ In European countries, the cattle were either driven between two such fires or over the ashes on their way to the Summer pastures, to ensure their yield. In days past, this was also the time in Australia when cattle were moved up to the high plains but, because of ecological concerns, this does not happen until mid-December. Bonfires are sometimes illegal by this time but the cattle can still be blessed with ashes from the Beltane fires.

✤ While crops are yet to mature in some parts of the country, in others, the hot, dry weather means that the natural food supply is falling off. It is a good time to make a ritual offering to Earth, giving thanks and asking for her continued provision. Some women offer a libation of their moonflow, the sign of their ability to create life. Others may be more comfortable offering the skin kept from the first fruit, or planting a tree – so long as something is given back.

The Love Festival

- ❊ Traditionally, the Aboriginal clans of North East Victoria and the Upper Murray regions met together at the Murray river near Albury where the annual floods had resulted in an abundance of food, before climbing into the high plains for the Summer months where they would feast on the Bogong moth. It was a time of social interaction and trade. Now, in early November, Aboriginals and other Australians come from as far as the Daintree and Alice Springs for Ngan-Girra, the Festival of the Bogong Moth – a weekend of story-telling, art, music, dance, and trade.

- ❊ There are a number of games associated with this festival: skimming the water from the wells of prosperous neighbours for luck; shooting a ball through a decorated hoop to represent the Sun moving through the heavens; leaping over creeks to give thanks for the water while praying that it continues to flow through Summer. Maids can increase their fairness by washing their faces in the dew from Beltane morn.

- ❊ Hawthorn blossoms at the beginning of Summer and is considered a tree of hope, pleasure and protection.* There is a custom that warns against sitting under a hawthorn on Beltane, because the veils between the worlds are thin and the fairies may put the unwary under a spell.

- ❊ The Love Festival celebrates sexuality and fertility** and when couples joined together on the night of the Beltane fires, their unions were called the greenwood marriages. It is Maia's feast, the Greek and Roman goddess who rules the forces of growth

---

* The hawthorn is also a noxious weed in some localities so be careful not to introduce or spread it to areas which have not previously had contact.

** Respecting Earth begins with self-respect. A loving reminder to her children, please employ safe sex practices.

and warmth, including sexual heat. Maia is the oldest and most beautiful of the Seven Sisters who form the constellation of the Pleaides. In ancient times, when the Sun and the Pleaides were in conjunction, it signalled the onset of fine weather and smooth sailing. This meant it was time for soldiers to start campaigning again, with a night of sexual revelry beforehand in case they died in battle, thus sowing the seed of their immortality in the womb of some fair maid.

※ The dance of the Maypole represents the sexual union of the Summer Lord with the Earth Mother, and the flowering of life. Coloured ribbons are attached to a hoop that is placed as high as possible. Taking a greenwood sapling for the maypole in feudal times was a public demonstration of the people's right to take wood at will. With the depletion of trees across the planet, it may be more appropriate to either find a living tree that will not be damaged by the process of the dancing and ribbons, or re-use a pole from another year. A bike wheel can be an effective fixture on top of a pole. Participants choose their ribbons, different colours having different connotations, and dance around the pole, weaving under and over each other until the ribbons are woven together. The final pattern formed by the woven ribbons can be used to divine the pattern of the coming year.

※ It is a people's day, when social hierarchies are put aside (Mayday has even become International Labour Day). Beltane baskets, decorated with Hawthorn blossom and leaves were filled with fruit or other sweet foods and given to the elderly, the sick, single parents, or any who were struggling.

※ Children took empty baskets around and received gifts from the householders, not as charity but as an offering made for the prosperity of the giver. It is a similar practice to trick-or-

The Love Festival

treating, a tradition that belongs to Hallowe'en as celebrated in the Northern hemisphere on 31 October.

✤ While it is becoming increasingly popular in Australia to celebrate Hallowe'en at the end of October with trick-or-treating and ghoulish parties, it bears no seasonal connection as it does on the other side of the world. However, Celtic mythology says that twice a year, at Samhain and Beltane, the veil between the world grows thin and people and spirit beings can pass through. Perhaps the celebration of Hallowe'en at the end of October is a chance for Euro-Australians to reach back into their old world and find their roots in this ancient and well-loved tradition.

✤ Similarly, the Hindu festival of Diwali is an early Autumn festival celebrated at the end of the monsoon season in India, but in Australia this places it around October/November. It is an explosion of light and colour, with fireworks and gift-giving and explosions of colour. Increasingly the celebrations spill over into the local street. If you are close to such a community that is celebrating this victory of light over darkness, and which invokes the blessings of the gods, it fits well with the ambience of the Love Festival.

✤ A tradition that originated in Germany is the Oktoberfest, a week of celebration and revelry that began with a horse race to celebrate a royal wedding in 1810. It became an annual event with beer and food tents until the beer became more popular than the horse-racing and tents even appeared on the race track. The horses were moved aside to make room for the beer.

✤ In Australia, there's still room for the horses with the Melbourne Cup, which takes place annually on the first Tuesday in November when the nation (and people in many other countries) stops for three and a half minutes to watch twenty-two thoroughbreds race the two-mile (3200m) handicap. It is also in keeping with Labour Day traditions, being a horse race where social divisions are equalised as the Aussie battler comes through while the favourite is last past the post. The Cup Eve parties with the Calcutta Sweep, the chicken and champagne breakfasts, and the fashions on the field are all part of the social rituals of the day.

- During the Burning Times from the 14th to the 17th century, European women were burnt as witches if they were seen as creative, sexual and wise. In Germany, the festival that marked the beginning of Summer was known as Walpurgishnacht, a night when 'witches' mounted their broomsticks to fly to a night of sexual abandon. The broomstick is an obvious phallic symbol and sometimes seen as a symbol of patriarchal oppression, but can also be seen as a symbol of sexual union with the ash rod thrust into the nest of birch. It is also possible that women 'rode' them in the fields to bless the crops.

- Medieval recipes for 'flying ointment' contained such poisonous substances as henbane, deadly nightshade, foxglove and aconite. In the correct measurement, these hallucinogenic ointments are capable of inducing a trance-like sleep. After using the concoctions, some people have reported dreams of flight and sexual revelry. The use of flying ointment is dangerous. A massage with perfumed oils is also reputed to cause a trance-like state and induce feelings of astral projection without the risk of hallucinogenic substances.

- In the spirit of Walpurgishnacht, in bold pronouncement of their sexuality and wisdom, women across the world have effectively taken the broomsticks from the closets and transformed them by taking part in Reclaim the Night marches.

The Love Festival

These demonstrations have continued since 1976, when 10 000 women took to the streets of Rome to protest against the sexual abuse of women and children.

❊ The Love Festival is a time for celebrating and respecting sexuality. For those who have been abused, it can become a time of healing and empowerment. Fire, now representing creative will and purification instead of fear, is an important part of the Reclaim the Night celebrations. As is belly-dancing, a dance-form with particular significance for women because it is closely associated with women's mysteries and has beneficial effects upon the reproductive system.

The Love Festival is a time for heightened awareness of fertility, of warmth and growth, of life. It is a time to celebrate our sexuality – remembering the rules of safe sex – and Earth's promised abundance. We have moved beyond the innocence of Spring into maturity, ready to cope with whatever the Summer may throw our way.

Summer Solstice
22 December

 *Sunwyse*

The Wheel turns ... Summer's strength, blistering, blazing, raising passions. Fruits ripen and crops turn to gold ...

The Summer Solstice is the longest day of the year, occurring between the 20 and 23 of December. Everywhere on this continent, the heat is oppressive and intense. In some places dry and thirsty, in others stormy and wet. Native fruit falls from bush and tree; wild gooseberry and passion fruit, acacia, dropping to the ground and scattering its seed over the arid land as supplication for a fertile future.

> *Eingana, Snake Mother of all, watches the animals move closer to the diminishing billabong. Fat snakes and lizards, and birds. She watches the people sink into the water's brackish coolness, and warns the crocodile to stay away from the piccaninnies. Sun-kissed women wade through the water, pulling water-lilies out for their flavoursome roots. Others sit by the edge, near Eingana, and make bark sandals to protect their feet from the burning ground. Dragonflies perform their intricate dances across the water's surface, wings shimmering in the light.*

> *Once welcome for his seductive warmth, Sun's touch now sears Eingana's brown flesh. She gathers the brittle twigs and begins to weave them into a Sun-Wheel, effigy of the one whose love has become so intense and all-consuming. The kulparti, Dreamtime snakes, rise from the waters and lay across the sky in thin streamers of cloud, stretching out as far as they can.*

> *The shamans of the red man walk to the four directions, gathering the snakes and bringing them to the sanctified space. Carefully the shamans caress the snakes, bathing them, blessing them, taking them into their mouths, dancing in unison with the sacred reptiles.*

By the water's edge, the pregnant black snakes draw together, caressing each other, writhing ecstatically in a tangled ball of glistening black scales and smooth red underbellies. Before they draw apart to birth their young, a shaman in feathered head-dress reaches into their midst and draws out a hard glass ball, the glain, the sacred egg which contains the wisdom of the philosophers.

Eingana cries out as the snakes birth their babies, and her cry moves across the deep waters, waking the Rainbow Serpent. He rises into the sky, his tongue flickering lightning across a flammable land; thunder following in his wake.

Eingana sends the Sun-Wheel spinning towards the serpent, where it flares and burns, dropping sparks upon the dry bush. She watches as the flames flare, springing upwards, consuming all in their eagerness. Finally, the serpent, too, is devoured and the clouds break open. Eingana smiles as she feels the rain soak through her and into Earth.

Pilgrims and refugees from the heat fill the roadways, joining with family and friends as they seek the coolness of mountain climes and the freshness of sea-breezes. Bottlenose dolphins cavort through the waves with their nursing offspring, to the delight of the white-skinned children adorned in zinc war paint, lurid green and pink and orange.

Evening draws down as they gather in open places and sing ancient words that promise the arrival of a sacred king, one who will bring a rule of peace and goodwill to Earth's children. They raise candles in offering to the stars and watch as the lights are reflected in the eyes of children.

When those same eyes grow bleary and begin to droop in sleep, a red-suited man flies high above, bringing a wind from the icy lands, a promise that Sun's harshness is about to decline. It is met by a wind

 *Sunwyse*

from the Hopi mesas, carrying a message from the Kachina father to the kachinas, the bringers of rain.

"Take with you our humble prayer ... for our people and people everywhere ... for all the animals, the birds and insects, and the growing things ... Take our message to the four corners of Earth, that all life may receive renewal ... May you go on your way with happy hearts and grateful thoughts."*

---

*Campbell, J., Historical Atlas of World Mythology Vol II: The Way of the Seeded Earth; Harper and Row Publishers, NY; 1989

Ways of Celebrating:

* Faerie magick is strong on this night and should be treated with great respect, but when the coolness of the evening comes down it is fine time for fun. Carrying a sprig of rue in a pocket, staying on a ley-line, crossing a running stream of water or turning a jacket inside out will protect against being led astray by the faerie. (Some people believe that faerie magick belongs to Europe but there are others convinced that the faeries joined the migrants and now share Australia with all the other multicultural and indigenous entities.)

* With the Sun's strength at its highest, the oil of herbs is most concentrated if harvested at this time and there are many traditions associated with their potency. St John's wort is considered to have protective powers, repelling evil. Yarrow placed under the pillow is said to bring dreams of future husbands; ferns gathered at midnight give invisibility. A hazel branch cut on Midsummer's Eve will lead to hidden treasure. Every region has its natural medicines that can be harvested now, but many have an unexpected potency and must be treated with care and respect.

* With the imminent decline of the Sun's strength from this day forward until the Winter Solstice, it is time to walk the boundaries of the townships and ward them against any ill-will that might creep in with the encroaching darkness. Singing, ringing bells, playing instruments, laughing and dancing are all effective means to keep negative energies at bay.

* In some European traditions, a huge Sun-Wheel was made and set aflame, then sent rolling down the hill to mark the end of the

Sun God's time and affirm the belief in his return. Obviously this is an inappropriate practice for our fire-prone country but the concept can be adapted. Sun-Wheels or effigies of the SunLord can be made and burnt in ritual fires, within the guidelines of the fire authorities, or buried in the Earth.

* A Native American tradition makes solar Wheels as amulets that protect the house or general areas. The Sun-Wheel is made, on Midsummer's Day, using vines. It is an equilateral cross within a circle representing four solar holidays and the four seasons. Feathers or yellow ribbons are tied to the point where the lines of the cross intersect, the point of power. They are also tied to the points where the arms of the cross intersect with the circle. When the Sun-Wheel is made, it is hung in the window and the old one is taken down and buried.

* The height of Summer is a time to seek the sea-breezes, the mountain heights, and the cool waterways. The heat slows down most things and sitting on a verandah with friends sinking a few stubbies, or having a picnic down by the river, are highly appropriate activities. But be wary of stone circles; it is said that the person who spends the night of Midsummer's Eve in a stone circle, if they survive, becomes mad or a great poet.

* St Nicholas' Day is celebrated on the 6 December. As a historical figure, St Nicholas was renowned for his generosity and goodness, consequently becoming the patron saint of Russia, Moscow, Greece, children, sailors, prisoners, bakers, pawnbrokers, shopkeepers and wolves. As perhaps one of the most universal personaes, his cult has evolved into one that emphasizes generosity and goodwill, and crosses both religious and cultural divides. Though his costume is hardly

Summer Solstice

appropriate to Midsummer in Australia, its familiarity makes it one of those things happily borne for the sake of a cherished tradition.

❋ Visitation of the sick, works of healing, sharing of wealth, support of the dying and the care of children in need were particular aspects of St Nicholas' ministry that are especially noted at this time. Of course, do not forget to leave out some food and drink on Christmas Eve in thanks for his generosity.

❋ Christmas, celebrating the birth of the Christian messiah, is celebrated on 25 December. Although Australians do not tend to follow the Northern hemispherical tradition of the twelve days which extend from Christmas to the Epiphany on 6 January, communal festivities do seem to extend from a week before Christmas when school breaks for the holidays until New Year's Day on 1 January.

❋ Traditional activities such as gift-giving, lavish home decorating, the singing of carols and sending of Christmas cards, all help to create a sense of community cohesion at a time when the heat tends to fray tempers. The Christmas wreath is a sign of welcome and mistletoe in the doorways is a symbol of good luck; a kiss beneath the mistletoe is a pledge of friendship.

❋ Though many of the Northern hemisphere's traditions have a firm hold, a number of people are moving away from the hot roast in the middle of the day to the more practical salads and barbecues. In celebration of the Earth's fruitfulness at this time, a bowl of fruit or some golden wine and honeycakes can be shared.

❇ Decorating a tree with tinsel recalls the legend where a poor widow who was distressed at being unable to give her family a beautifully decorated Christmas tree. While she slept the spiders wove webs through the tree, which turned to silver when she woke. Rather than cutting down a tree, perhaps acquire a living tree which can then be planted out afterwards or decorate one that is already outside.

❇ It is a difficult time of the year for many, who cannot afford to give as they would like, or are alienated from friends and family, or suffering other misfortune. Various traditions are developing that recognise such people as an integral part of community life. These include the Motorcycle Riders' Association toy run, community Christmas parties, and wishing trees.

❇ Candles represent the eternal light. Burning them at a time when the Sun's strength has peaked and is about to begin declining is like a final tribute. The Jewish eight day festival of Hanukkah occurs on the 25th day of the Jewish month of Kislev, which places it at the time of the new moon closest to the Winter Solstice in the Northern hemisphere but closest to the Summer Solstice in Australia. Hannukkah celebrates the re-dedication of the temple in Jerusalem following a victory over the Maccabees over 2000 years ago. For eight nights, a candle is added to the menorah at sunset to commemorate the eight days that oil was burned in the temple. Similar to the Christmas activities, Hanukkah involves family celebration and gift-giving.

❇ Boxing Day on 26 December began as a day when the apprentices broke open the boxes to which their employers had been contributing during the year. There was also a tradition

Summer Solstice

were alms boxes were broken open and the money distributed to the poorer members of the community.

❃ Summer Solstice, mingled with the Christmas celebrations, is a time of mixed emotions for most people. The days and nights are crowded with social and familial activity even while the heat saps energy and enthusiasm as though it were water evaporating from the land. There is a sense of relief in knowing that, as the Wheel turns, the Sun's fierceness will diminish and there will be a time for going inward again. Yet there is also pleasure in knowing there are still plenty of days ahead to enjoy the reign of the light.

The Harvest Feast
2 February

Sunwyse

The Wheel turns...first harvest. Life is affirmed in Earth's bounty. Sweaty bodies test their strength and vigour...

First harvests are done, the last sheaf of wheat cut down, and there is time to gather together before beginning on the next harvest. It is a time of abundance, when Earth overflows with her generosity. It is a time for feasting, on the grains and fruits, with berry pies and apple cider. Also known by the Celtic name of Lughnasadh, this festival is calculated 92 days after the Love Festival, working on a calendar of 365 days where the other cross-quarter festivals are held at the transition from one month to the next. With the Sun still high, this festival has a strong masculine ambience.

> *A dark-skinned man pulls himself up the massive tree using vines and limbs. In the tree-tops, he tests the weight of the huge bunya nut in his palm. It is easily the size of his head, and approaching ripeness, but not quite ready to be plucked. When he returns to the ground, he grins and nods to the waiting men.*
>
> *The message stick passes into the runner's hand. It tells them to come, the harvest will be good and all who can travel should come to the feast.*
>
> *The messengers race away, light-footed and quick as they flicker like shadows through the rainforest. They go to the coast, the mountains, the plains. Everywhere their news is welcomed and people, large groups and small, move towards the mountain and anticipate the feasting. A giant eagle glides across the sky, leading the way.*
>
> *Lugh, all robed in red and with his beautiful face shining like the Sun, looks down on the people in the valley standing around the group on horseback. He raises his long arm high against the sky and lets it drop again to his side. His clarion voice echoes across the valley, bouncing back from the hills.*
>
> *"Let the games begin!"*

Shyly the maidens lean over the railings and, from beneath lowered lids, watch the glistening bodies of the young men as they wrestle one another, strain manfully in the tug o' war, and race around the oval.

The way is cleared for the main event and voices grow hoarse with cheering as the horses and their riders tear down the hills, through the narrow river crossings, up the mountain ridge, dodging trees and wombat holes and other competitors. Neck to neck they come racing down the final stretch, bodies extended and the crowd cheering them faster.

Last year's winner is displaced, cut down in his prime like the last sheaf of wheat in the paddock. Sadly, he hands over his crown to the younger victor and turns away, stumbling a little as he walks down from the stage.

The cowbell sounds and they begin to drift towards the old walnut tree. A number have already gathered, young and old, city dwellers and mountain men, mothers and children. They listen as the poems are given, telling of their heritage, of heroes and fools, strong horses, loyal dogs, obstacles overcome, laughter and sadness. The young men wonder if such poems will ever be written about their adventures.

Apart from the festivities, the Elders gather. Quietly the pipe is passed around the circle, and their breath is united. Now, only truth may be spoken as they debate the needs of the people, the laws to be changed, new directions to be taken.

Silence falls as an old but still upright man stands at the door.

"By what right do you approach this council?"

He does not hesitate in reply. "By right of the council's invitation."

"Why would you sit with this council?"

"That I may offer the wisdom of my years to our people."

"Then, enter and be welcome."

As evening draws down over the mountain, the brown-skinned woman strikes the bunya nuts with sharp stones and places them in the fire. Others put in their contribution: a large possum; a couple of snakes; some turkey eggs; wild yams and grubs. And the succulent figs.

Bellies full, they join the neighbouring clan for a corroboree. Tall, thin warriors marked with stark white clay and red ochre circle around the fire and begin to dance their stories to the beat of clap-stick and the long hum of didgeridoo.

As the Sun rises, a priestess takes a silken cord and binds it first around the left wrist of the maiden, then about the left wrist of the young man. "For a year and a day," she intones. "You are bound to each other. For a year and a day, at which time you will decide to part or be the closer bound."

The young couple clasp each other's hand, and the silken tie feels soft against their skin. They are called from their wondering by the laughter of friends, who hold ready the broom. Hands still clasped, they leap it high, confident. The priestess hands it to them.

"The first gift towards setting up your home together." She grins at the Tailltean bride, who whispers quietly: "And perhaps it will carry me across the sky on Walpurgisnacht."

The best fighters among the clans issue their final challenges. Strong bodies clash against each other, arms locked together, feet tangled, heads knocking. As each is defeated, their clan gathers its belongings, and a supply of bunya nuts, and begins the long journey home. The feasting is done, the days grow ever shorter and it is time to prepare for a darkening time.

The Harvest Feast

Ways of Celebrating:

❉ Traditional fairs at harvest time were used by the medieval guilds to display their workmanship and today's harvest festivals usually include a craft market and displays of various skills and talents. When looking for events that celebrate the pageantry and excess of the first harvests, a good example is Sydney's Gay Mardi Gras, involving a month-long round of activity, and the Chinese New Year, on the February new moon.

❉ The Australia Day Weekend, commemorating the landing of the English on Australian shores in 1788, sees a variety of community events taking place, including athletic carnivals, craft markets and harvest festivals. Each region has its native harvests that come in at different times and sometimes celebrations can be tailored around these e.g. earlier in this century, the Aboriginals of SE Queensland gathered for the Bunya Nut festival between January and March and, depending on the bounty of the Bunya nuts, they would invite neighbouring tribes to join them.

❉ The masculine energy is at a height at this time of the year, and there is an athletic emphasis with team games, demonstrations of skill and strength, horsemanship trials, wrestling and mountain-climbing. Such hard work always needs to be followed by a feast and, at this time of the year, that should include grains, fruit, beer and cider.

❉ It is an appropriate time for paying homage to heroes with prize-giving, award presentations, poetry and song. The Mountain Cattlemans' Association, of the High Plains, hold their annual heritage festival late in January, with horse-racing, novelty events, bush skills and story-telling.

❁ The spirit of the corn is cut down, and so it also a time of death and commemoration. As loaves are made from the first grain, corn dollies are made from the last. When the last sheath is still standing, the men take turns throwing their sickles at it until it is knocked down. At the feasting later, the victor is honoured and the corn dolly consigned to the fire or buried in the Earth to show that the SunLord's time is done. Corn necklaces are made, with their promise of life to be renewed in the spring.

❁ While the communities are gathered together, it is a good opportunity for Councils of Elders to sit and debate the needs of their communities. Laws are made and revised, alliances are formed for the coming year. In our modern society, this takes shape more often in the annual general meetings of community organisations. Not as popular an activity as wrestling or feasting but an essential and timely one.

❁ Elders tend to be unrecognised in modern communities. They are the wise ones, grandparents, teachers, always ready to lend an ear or a bit of advice (even if it's unwanted). Public recognition should be made of their contribution to individuals, families, and communities.

❁ Lughnasadh was an opportunity for young people to wander around and select a spouse for a trial marriage of a year and a day, equating with thirteen lunar cycles. At the following Lughnasadh, these couples would then either confirm their commitment or walk away from each other, one to the North and one to the South, to demonstrate their parting. The romantic appeal of St Valentine's Day on 14 February encourages young lovers to give voice to their feelings and, with the rush of the Christmas season over and the almost-to-be-counted-on fine weather, it is considered a good time for marriages.

- The Harvest Feast is the culmination of the Summer activity, testing each other's strength, showing off skills and abilities, courting a spouse. It has a strong, vibrant spirit that encourages us to take control of our lives as the Wheel moves forward again.

Autumn Equinox
21 March

The Wheel turns...harvest, harvest's end. The Sun grows old and thoughts turn to the coming Winter. Earth's generosity is preserved, stored against the cold. Seeds, bulbs are set below Earth's surface...

Autumn Equinox is a time of balancing, for weighing what has been achieved and planning for what is to come, of reviewing directions and looking at what is needed in our lives. Fruit bowls overflow with colour and goodness, but the forces of darkness and light once more battle each other for supremacy. At the Autumn Equinox, they are still in balance but this time the Sun has grown weaker, older, and darkness will be victorious.

The cattlemen are reluctant to leave the lush grasslands of the high plains but they feel Winter's approach and head for the low-lands, driving the cattle in front. The stock are sleek and healthy, their coats gleaming. And the annual muster is a fine time, hard work but with good company and the fresh, crisp mountain air. As they descend towards the foothills and plains, the mountain men cast calculating eyes over the thick undergrowth and the diminished waterways, wondering when the rains will come. A pall of smoke hangs in the horizon; fire used now to prevent fire in the future.

A bush band performs on a stage adorned in sweetly smelling hops. A group of women are line-dancing to one side. Another woman sits at a table drawing sketches of the people, a carbon history of the event. Stalls offering wine and cheese line the square.

The sounds of a pipe band penetrate the lazy afternoon and people leave their seats to move towards the main street. Bright-coloured floats, decorated in flowers and fruits and hundreds of ribbons, form a slow moving parade. The occupants wave to family and friends that they see in the crowd. A clown on stilts throws lollies to the children.

Proudly, gloriously, the SunLord moves into the parade. He shines brighter than the golden chariot that carries him and his Harvest

Queen, the most beautiful maiden of all. Her dark hair is filled with starlight, her eyes reflect the changing colours of the sky. She is dressed in veils and flowers and her mouth curves in a smile of sweet satisfaction.

Dancing around them are old ladies and young men; fair-haired maidens and dark lords; children and elders. The crowds wave palm branches in greeting and raise their voices in a song of welcome.

As the parade moves through the town, the Shadows lengthen behind the chariot of the SunLord, mocking the light he carries. The crowd falls away, the floats are left standing beside the road, and people drift towards their homes. The trees and rocks take up the song, but the sweet notes are tinged with hungry pain.

The Harvest Queen cries out as the shadows swallow them and she loses sight of her Lord. In a last attempt to outshine the darkness, the SunLord casts the shadows aside and catches a brief glimpse of his teary-eyed lover before the darkness descends.

Battling with the shadows, he is knocked to the ground, feels them consume his life-force. They are the stronger and he falls into the open arms of Mother Earth as she welcomes him back to her embrace, to her womb.

The ShadowLord looks to the beautiful maiden who waits outside the entrance to the Underworld, where her lover has gone. She is Queen of the Shadows now, but will not look to him. He rolls away the stone covering the entrance and beckons her inside, into his world, his realm. Follow she must, but she will not take his hand.

Lungkata, the blue-tongued lizard, and Kuniya, the Woma python, have watched the pageant unfold. Now they follow, retreating into the Mother's embrace for the long rest.

 *Sunwyse*

Ways of Celebrating:

- ❈ Celebrating the harvest is a prime focus of this time with winery walkabouts and other harvest festivals. While a harvest feast can easily be conducted at home, it is also fun to join in community festivals with their street parades and markets displaying the productive nature of diverse community groups. Such multicultural gatherings acknowledge the agricultural harvest while also recognising the physical, spiritual, emotional, and historical gains that have been made.

- ❈ Our multicultural heritage is an important part of our individual identity and that of the Australian society. Folk-dances, traditional feasts, singing, story-telling, and visits to the old family homes are ways of reconnecting with this heritage and making it real for our children. St Patrick's Day on 17 March is a celebration of the Irish influence upon Australian culture.

- ❈ Harvests are very much a gamble in Australia's unpredictable climate. The lack of water reminds us of the need for conservation and careful planning, and preparations are made for the on-coming Winter. There is jam making and preserves, as well as crafts such as weaving and the making of apple-headed dolls.

- ❈ In colder climates, this festival was a time of preparing for the Winter, and included hunting of wild animals and killing the weaker domestic stock who were unlikely to make it through the cold. Rituals are enacted to communicate with animal spirits and guides as a way to deepen awareness and honour the animals whose lives are given for the sustenance of others. Such rituals are best conducted by an experienced teacher but telling stories about animals, writing poetry, drawing pictures and, of course, spending time with them, are all ways of connecting with their spirits. If fishing or hunting are undertaken, there should be some act of thanksgiving for the animal, which can be as simple as saying a prayer before eating the meal.

- There are many myths associated with this time of passage from the light-filled days to the dark cold season with a preparation for rebirth. These can be re-enacted and experienced on a personal level through such activities as prayer vigils, Native American sweat lodges, or any rituals of purification.

- The Jewish Passover or Pesach sees a thorough cleansing and the removal of all leaven from the house. The traditional Passover meal remembers a time when the Jewish people escaped from slavery in Egypt and began their journey through the desert. This takes place in the Jewish month of Nissan, generally around the full moon which follows the equinox.

- Palm Sunday, on the weekend preceding Easter, has become a day for peace marches, asking for temperance and balance, for tolerance, in the World.

- The Catholic celebration of Easter takes place on the first Sunday after the full moon after the Equinox. It begins with a period of denial in the 40-day lenten season extending from Ash Wednesday to Easter, which commemorates the death and resurrection of the Christian messiah. It ends with an excessive indulgence in chocolate eggs, a carry-over from the older rites celebrating the renewal of Spring (Easter is a Spring-time festival in the Northern hemisphere). The equal-armed cross on hot cross buns is an ancient symbol representing the balanced Sun.

- Demonstrating a faith in the Sun's eventual return, paddocks are ploughed and the soil turned over. Offerings are made to Earth of yarn, seeds, tobacco or any harvest product. Planting bulbs can signify a descent to the Underworld with the promise of return come the Spring.

The Sun's reign is over. The nights grow longer and darkness settles in for the duration. As the Wheel turns, thoughts move away from what has been and towards the dark side of the year.

Festival of the Dead
30 April

The old year dies as a weakening Sun spends less and less time bringing light and warmth to Earth. In Winter's darkness, beneath Earth's surface, the seed lies dormant, resting, waiting...

Also known by the Celtic name of Samhain, this festival is celebrated in Australia from the evening of 30 April to the evening of the next day. It is most commonly known as Hallowe'en, which falls at the end of October in the Northern hemisphere. The last of Earth's bounty has been gathered, plants die back, deciduous trees shed their brilliant Autumn colours and gum trees shed their bark, curling down their trunks to expose the smooth silver skin beneath to the Sun's diminished rays. Winter begins.

> *In the dim pre-dawn, they come like spectres from another time. Frail old men dressed in hats and ties, with spit-polished shoes. Some come in wheelchairs, some stand alone, some lean heavily on the arm of a family member. On their jacket breasts are the bronze and silver medals, the brightly coloured ribbons, the badges that tell a story of pain, loss, and victory.*
>
> *A monument, like an ancient cairn, stands silhouetted against the lightening sky. The stone-like faces of the men watch as the names of the dead grow slowly visible. A sole trumpeter plays the mournful notes of the "Last Post", breaking the silence but not the stillness.*
>
> *A chaplain stands before the monument and faces them.*
>
> *"They shall not grow old, as we that are left grow old.*
> *Age shall not weary them, nor the years condemn.*
> *At the going down of the Sun And in the morning –*
> *We will remember them."*

Festival of the Dead

There is no hesitation in the response echoed by old and young across the continent.

"We will remember them!"

Those who are able turn to the streets and march together again, remembering the days when they marched between the worlds of life and death, fighting demons from both.

Then, to the place reserved for the returned soldiers, to share a cup and spin a yarn, and... watch the pennies spin.

"Tails!" Laughter and groans. Money drawn in and placed out. The coins tossed into the air again. For these returned servicemen and women, life has always included a strong element of chance.

A mother nervously glances at the Winter landscape; bare trees stand silhouetted against the Sun that sets so early. The paddocks, with their soil turned, look strangely barren. The silent gums on the hillside watch the darkness come. A dingo howls and the mother draws a rune of protection over the entrance as she hastens the children indoors and closes the door against the night.

Inside, friends and family fill the house with cheerful talk. A well-stoked fire keeps everybody warm and the smells of cooking waft temptingly through the house. The food is laid out on the table and, as each takes their seat for the Fleadh nan Mairbh, the Feast of the Dead, the house grows silent again. A chair is left empty though food is piled on the plate set before it.

Outside, the light drains away from the world and the night becomes mist-filled, as though all is seen through an eerily-glowing veil. Shades, insubstantial, move back and forth through the mist. They hover, testing the veil's permeability, seeming unsure of this freedom to leave their familiar domain.

Suddenly the shades grow still, suspended in time. Then they move apart, bowing low for the Cailleach, the Veiled One. Red teeth, matted white hair and a far-seeing eye in the middle of her blue-black face; still, she is beloved of many. The Cailleach raises high her mighty hammer and strikes the ground, rendering it hard and cold as iron.

As at a signal, the beings of the Otherworld surge forward through the veil. This night is theirs. They are the faerie, the devas, the angels. They are the gods and goddesses, the ghosts and goblins. They are the ancestors and those yet to be born.

Hecate, Queen of Witches, walks the roads with her hounds. She will wander until the feasting is done, then wait at the crossroads for those who offer the meal's leftovers to her hounds. If pleased with their offering, Hecate may grant whatever they dare ask.

The Morrigan, the Death-hag, straddles the river of her urination and waits for the Dagda, the Good God, to join her in a night of lovemaking. Those who overhear their conversation may learn of the souls to be carried away in the coming year.

The dead visit their family homes and watch as the table is set, laden with the food of a plentiful harvest. When a place is set for them, they whisper into the silence, whisper of secrets learned in the Otherworld.

Two boys, almost men, sidle towards the door. Their mother is talking with a cousin and her face is turned away. The boys make their escape and run, muffling laughter, to meet with mates under the old peppercorn.

But no-one is waiting, only the shadows. When a grunt sounds in the bushes beside them, the boys jump, and mock each other's timidity. The other boys start to arrive – it's not always easy to escape a mother's watchful eye.

"Who's first?" says one.

No one steps forward. The shadows stretch longingly towards them and a possum growls from the trees across the road.

"I'm game!" The lad who speaks holds himself tall and wipes his palms down the sides of his trousers. He lines up, takes a deep breath, and races off down the road. Shades follow him, swift ghouls and hungry goblins close upon his heels.

When the boy is out of sight, the next in line takes off, daring the darkling creatures to catch him by the heel. When all have completed the circuit, the boys meet again by the tree. But the first boy to take to the road has not reappeared. Anxiously the friends peer into the darkness, and wonder how they dared challenge the powers of the night.

The boy springs up before them, face distorted and growling like a demon. In the struggle that follows, their tensions fall away.

"Seachain á taibshe, watch out for the ghosts," cries one as they approach their homes.

The taibshe, garishly masked, are just leaving the homes. The boys are glad to have been absent when these strange ones were invading their homes, rearranging ornaments and making mockery of the silent people within. Back in their homes, the boys join in the board games and listen as stories are told, as songs are sung and poems recited, as people recall the old ways and plan the new.

 *Sunwyse*

Ways to Celebrate:

❅ The Festival of the Dead is a time of haunting darkness, a time for remembering that the dead are still part of our present and our future. Visiting cemeteries or other memorial sites with the children, placing flowers in remembrance, and telling the ancestral stories, are important rituals of family identification and continuity. From the dawn service at shrines reminiscent of Celtic stone cairns to the parade of surviving soldiers, the ANZAC day activities, on 25 April, are well in the Samhain spirit.

❅ It is not a time to be alone. The 'Fleadh nan Mairbh' or 'Feast of the Dead' is a family meal where places are also set for those members who have passed over, inviting them to join the feasting. The meal is shared in silence so the spirits can tell their secrets and reawaken ancient memories. A candle or lantern can be placed in the window to help wandering spirits find their way home.

❅ At Samhain, the veil between the worlds is thin and strange entities are abroad. Hecate, Queen of the Witches, is reputed to walk the night with her hounds. Leftovers from the meal can be laid at the triple crossroads for her hounds and, if she feels favourably inclined, Hecate may grant the wish of the supplicant.

❅ Some use this night to consult the tarot cards or the runes, or any method of divination. Others find it more appropriate to offer prayers for the departed souls and for the living.

Festival of the Dead

- The custom of 'trick or treating' grew from the belief that souls who were not prayed for would play tricks on people during Samhain. In the Northern hemisphere, children dress in ghoulish costumes and go from door-to-door offering the householder a choice between a trick or a treat.

- Older boys test their bravery and demonstrate their manly courage by venturing outside and undertaking various challenges to prove they are not afraid of the darkling forces. This energy can be harnessed by performing rites of transition for boys entering adulthood. These can be elaborate traditional ceremonies or simple expeditions to the bush for a father-to-son discussion.

- This festival marks the end of the harvest and anything left on the vine, in the vegetable patch or in the paddocks after this time will have been blighted by the faeries, rendered unfit for human consumption, and should be left to decompose.

At the Festival of the Dead, past and future are present in the one time. It is a night for telling stories of the past and discussing dreams for the future. As Winter begins, thoughts turn towards an inner world. It is a time of rest, reflection, and waiting for the Wheel to turn again.

Glossary and Bibliography

ABORIGINAL	– from Latin: *Ab* meaning *from* or *out of*; *origin* meaning *source* or *beginning*; and *al* meaning *one belonging to*. – capitalised to demonstrate difference to the aboriginal people of other lands.
AUTUMN EQUINOX	– also known as: Alban Eleud, *the Light of the Water*; Second Harvest or Harvest Home; or Mabon, a Cymric term which may mean the *son of Modron, the Great Mother* or *Great Son* or *Great Hunter*.
BELTANE	– Anglicised version of the Irish Gaelic, Bealtine (pronounced *bee-YAWL-tinnuh*) meaning 'bright fire' or 'Bel-fire' and referring to Bel, the Celtic god of light.
BRAT BHRIDE	– Irish Gaelic for *Brighid's mantle* and referring to a piece of cloth left outside for the Imbolc period i.e. from sundown to sundown and kept in the house for the following year as protection. Reputedly useful as a headache remedy.
BRIDEOG	– representation, made from sheaf of oats or straw/rushes and dressed in women's clothing, of Celtic goddess, Brighid.
CAILLEACH	– Irish Gaelic: *veiled one* and pronounced *coy luck*. Refers to the death crone aspect of the Goddess.
CAIRNS	– burial mounds piled high with stones.
THE CALCUTTA	– sweepstakes conducted on Melbourne Cup Eve in which each horse is auctioned off to the highest bidder.
CELTIC	– from *Keltoi*, the name given to the indigenous people of central Europe by the Greeks – descended from ancient Indo-European race that once extended from the Baltic Sea to West Ireland. Term generally applied to Cymric, Cornish, Manx, Irish Gaels, Scottish Gaels and Bretons.
CRONE	– someone who has attained the third age of woman, a menopausal time of new freedom where life's lessons are transmuted into wisdom.
CYMRIC	– refers to inhabitants of Wales. *Welsh* was a derogatory Anglo-Saxon term for *wog*.

Glossary

DIES NATALIS INVICTI	– the Birthday of the Unconquered Sun decreed in 274 by the Roman emperor Aurelian and celebrated until 323 when it was Christianised by Constantine.
DIVINATION	– reading by clairvoyance or other intuitive abilities that which is hidden from ordinary sight, including possibilities for the future.
EASTER	– a Christian celebration commemorating the death and resurrection of Jesus, generally celebrated on the first Sunday after the first 'ecclesiastical' full moon after the Northern hemisphere's Spring Equinox. It is calculated by Roman Catholic tradition from 21 March Gregorian, and by Orthodox tradition from 21 March Julian which equates currently with 3 April Gregorian. In Roman Catholic tradition, if the first full moon after the equinox falls upon a Sunday, then Easter is calculated for the following Sunday. In this way, it avoids falling on the same date as the Jewish Passover.
ECCLESIASTICAL	– when referring to full moon, the fourteenth day of the lunar cycle.
EPIPHANY	– Greek word signifying a manifestation or revelation. The Feast of the Epiphany celebrated on 6 January commemorates the manifestation of Jesus to the three kings.
EQUINOX	– equal hours of day and night; as the Earth takes about 365.26 day to circle the Sun, the date and time of the equinox may shift each year.
GREENWOOD	– refers to the sexual unions formed at Beltane.
GREGORIAN	– refers to post-1582 calendar, established by Pope Gregory XIII to replace the Julian calendar. It had 12 months per year with an average of 365.2425 days per year. Established in countries with a predominantly Catholic government in 1582 with the elimination of 10 days. Instituted in the non-Catholic countries of Britain and her colonies in 1752 with the elimination of 12 days.
GUILD	– group of people dedicated to mastering a common skill/craft.

HALLOWE'EN	– the eve of All Hallows or All Saints day and said to be the time when unsanctified spirits are abroad.
HANUKKAH	– Hebrew word meaning *dedication*.
HILL'S HOIST	– patented style of free-wheeling clothes line.
HOPI	– indigenous desert people of North America.
IMBOLC	– Irish Gaelic: *In the belly* and pronounced *Im bul'k*.
JULIAN	– calendar established by Julius Caesar in 46BC. It had 12 months per year with an average of 365.25 days. Pre-dated the Gregorian calendar, established by Pope Gregory XIII in 1582.
KACHINA	– Hopi tradition: personified representations of life-energy who help the crops to grow and are responsible for the bringing of rain.
KRILL	– Atlantic shrimp-like crustacean.
LENTEN	– refers to period of Lent, the 40 days of sacrifice and/or fasting preceding the Christian Easter rituals and commemorating the 40 days which Jesus spent in the desert prior to commencing his ministry.
LUGHNASADH	– or Lughnasa, (pronounced loo-na-sah) takes its name from a Celtic deity by the name of Lugh. *Nasa* or *nasadh* is Irish Gaelic for commemoration and refers to the Games of Lugh which were held at this seasonal point in the Celtic calendar. The Scots Gaelic is Lunasda (pronounced loo-nus-duh) or Lunasdal (pronounced loo-nus-dal). The Manx is Laa Luanys or Laa Lunys.
MAIDEN	– first stage of a woman's life-cycle, from menarche to motherhood.
MAGICK	– the convention of this more archaic spelling distinguishes magick from the sleight-of-hand trickery used to pull rabbits out of a hat.
MAYDAY	– see Beltane
MENARCHE	– first moonflow

Glossary

MENORAH	– a candelabrum with several branches, used in Jewish ritual. The Menorah used during Hanukkah has nine branches.
MUMMERS	– performers in disguise, often dressed as the opposite sex or as animals, who spontaneously appear at community celebrations.
MOONFLOW	– menstruation.
NIRVANA	– final blissful stage of the soul's evolution in Buddhist tradition.
PAGAN	– from Roman *paganus* meaning *country-dweller*; a person who regards Earth and nature as sacred.
PICCANINNY	– from Aboriginal pidgin language, meaning a small child.
PRAYER-TIES	– from Native American Lakota, where offerings of tobacco or other herbs are twisted in a piece of cloth and tied together on a string, which is hung on trees and left until it opens and releases the offering.
QUICKENING	– the first sensation of a child moving within the womb.
ROMANY	– Gypsy.
RUNE	– symbol taken from the early Teutonic alphabet or *Futharc*, invested with magick.
SAMHAIN	– Irish Gaelic, pronounced *Sow'n* and meaning *Summer's End*.
SATURNALIA	– a Roman festival of several days duration commencing on 17 December with the first day dedicated to religious rites and the following two to seven days involving role reversal; gift giving; public gambling; closure of shops, and the closure of schools and law courts.
SHADE	– spectre.
SHAMAN	– Siberian word originally referring to a visionary able to cure the sick and locate animals for hunting. Contemporary use of the word sees it applied to priests/healers from various traditions reputedly able to travel into the spirit realm to find healing and insights for the tribe.

SIGIL	– symbolic representation, usually drawing, of a magickal principle.
SMITHCRAFT	– metalwork.
SMUDGE STICKS	– bundles of fragrant herbs, usually including sage and sweetgrass, used as purifying incense in Native American tradition.
SOLSTICE	– Latin: *sol* meaning *sun* and *sistene* meaning *to stop*. Refers to the longest and shortest days of the year when the Sun appears to stand still in the sky. As the Earth takes approximately 365.26 days to circle the Sun, the date and time of the solstices may vary from year to year.
SUMMER SOLSTICE	– also known as Litha (Norse or Anglo-Saxon for *longest day* and pronounced *leeta*); Midsummer.
SUNWYSE	– the direction of the Sun's movement across the sky during the course of the year. In the Southern hemisphere, this is North to South in an anti-clockwise direction.
SWEEP	– sweepstakes. A form of race betting in which the names of all the horses in a particular race are placed in a hat and drawn at random for each person who has paid an entry amount. This combined amount is divided up into the prize money.
TAIBSHE	– singular of *taibshi*, Irish Gaelic for *ghosts* and referring to cheeky spirits, represented by mummers, who enter people's houses at Samhain.
TAILLTEAN	– Tailltean is a place in Ireland where the Lughnasadh festivites were held and marriages were made for a year and a day.
TEUTONIC	– the Germanic peoples, including Scandinavians and Anglo-Saxons.

Glossary

WALBURG	– was reputedly the Goddess of Walpurgisnacht (May Eve) and represented at the celebrations through a May Queen. Roman Catholic legend maintains that she was an Englishwoman who became abbess of Heidenheim monastery during the eighth century, though no records exist of this monastery and its name translates as *home of heathens*.
WALPURGISHNACHT	– pronounced *vawl-PUR-gis-nakt* and meaning Walburg's night
WASSAIL	– from Anglo-Saxon *wes hal* meaning *to be whole*; to toast with hot ale or cider, from a maple-turned bowl.
YULE	– Norse: pronounced *yool* meaning *Wheel*. Relates to MidWinter.
YULETIDE	– the eve of Winter Solstice.

 *Sunwyse*

Bibliography

BOOKS

Lesley Antanoff; *Crystal Awareness*; Renascent, Nunawading; 1994

Harvey Arden; *Dreamkeepers*; HarperCollins, New York; 1994

Freya Aswynn; *Leaves of Yggdrasil*; Llewellyn Publications USA; 1990

Joseph Campbell; *Historical Atlas of World Mythology Vol II: The Way of the Seeded Earth Part 3: Mythologies of the Primitive Planters: The Middle and South Americas*; Harper and Row, New York, 1989

Barbara Ehrenreich and Deidre English; *Witches, Midwives and Nurses*; The Feminist Press; [NPND],1973

Gracie Green, Joe Tamacchi, Lucille Gill; *Tjarany Roughtail*; 2nd edition; Magabala Books Aboriginal Corporation; 1993

Janet and Stewart Farrar; *Eight Sabbats for the Witches*; Phoenix Publishing Inc USA; 1988

Sir James George Frazer; *The Golden Bough (abridged)*, first published as two volumes in 1890, Mary Douglas (ed.); George Rainbird Ltd; 1978 edition

Rosemary Ellen Guiley; *The Encyclopedia of Witches and Witchcraft*; Facts on File, New York; 1989

Rev. Hugo Hoever, S.O.Cist.: *Lives of the Saints*; 3rd edition; Catholic Book Publishing Co, New York; 1977

Ronald Hutton; *The Stations of the Sun – a history of the Ritual Year in Britain*; Oxford University Press, New York; 1996

Prudence Jones and Nigel Pennick; *A History of Pagan Europe*; Routledge, UK and USA; 1995

Eddie Kneebone; *A Koorie Experience* (video and accompanying notes); Wangaratta Centre for Adult Education, NPND

Bibliography

Norma Levine; *Buddhist Wisdom*; Goldsfield Press, UK; 1996

Alexander Macbain; *Celtic Mythology and Religion*; first edition 1917; Oracle Publishing Ltd, England; 1996

Caitlin Matthews; *The Celtic Book of Days*; Goldsfield Press Ltd; 1995

Geoffrey Parinder; *Asian Religions*, Sheldon Press, London; 1975

Caitlin Matthews; *The Celtic Tradition*; Element Books Ltd, UK; 1989

Patricia Monaghan; *Goddesses and Heroines*; Llewellyn Publications USA; 1981

Dr Daith OhOgain; *Myth, Legend and Romance – an Encyclopaedia of the Irish Folk Traditions*; Ryan Publishing Co Ltd, London; 1990

Lira Silbury; *The Sacred Marriage*; Llewellyn Publications, USA; 1994

Constance Campbell Petrie; *Tom Petrie's Reminiscences of Early Queensland*; University of Queensland Press; first published 1904 by Watson, Ferguson and Co.; 3rd edition, 1992

Stuart Piggott; *The Druids*; 2nd edition, Thames and Hudson, UK; 1975

Eirlys Richards; *Pinarri – Introducing Aboriginal Languages in Kimberley Schools*; Summer Institute of Linguistics, Australian Aborigines Branch, Darwin; 1987

Ninian Smart; *The World's Religions*; Cambridge University Press; 1989

Starhawk; *Dreaming the Dark*; Beacon Press USA; 1982

Starhawk; *The Spiral Dance*; Harpercollins New York; 1989

Paddy Slade; *Natural Magic*; Hamlyn Publishing Group Ltd, London; 1990

T W Rolleston; *The Illustrated Guide to Celtic Mythology*; Studio Editions Ltd; 1993

Barbara G. Walker; *The Woman's Encyclopaedia of Myths and Secrets*; Harper and Row Publishers Inc, New York; 1983

Herman Wouk; *This is my God*, Fontana; 1976

 *Sunwyse*

JOURNALS and NEWSPAPERS

Australia Productivity Council; *Days of Significance for Australia – the 1985 All-Australian Almanac;* Hodja Educational Resources Co-op Ltd; Richmond, Australia; 1984

Assembly of the Elder Troth; *Irminsul – Journal of the Northern Way;* Leumeah NSW; Vol 1: No 3, 1996

Assembly of the Elder Troth; *Why Á satrú?* Leumeah NSW; 1996

Maria Ceresa; *Rock that holds fingerprints of life;* the Australian newspaper; 25/9/1996

Padraigin Clancy; *"Seachain á Taibshe" Watch out for the Ghost*; Aisling magazine; Samhain 1992

Green Egg magazine Vol 27 No 107; *Interfaith Dialogue: Question #4; Lilinah bat-Anat;* Winter 1994-95

Peggy Hernon; *The Celts and Christianity;* Aisling Quarterly; August 1991

Caitlin Matthews; *News from the Lyceums;* Cesara Publications; S. Ireland; Isian News No. 8 Spring 1996

Optus; *A New Year of Celebrations – Desk Calendar;* 1997

Steven Posch; *I Chope you Chave a Chappy Chanuka;* Green Egg magazine Vol 27 No 107; Winter 1994-95

Ed Sellner; *Druids and Druidesses, Spiritual Leaders of the Celts*; The Aisling magazine; Uimhair 18

Uluru-Katu Tjuta National Park; *Anunga Language;* 1996

Uluru-Katu Tjuta National Park; *Non-Aboriginal History;* 1996

Uluru-Kata Tjuta National Park; *Understanding the Country;* 1996

Virginia Westbury; *Festivals and invocations – Australian style;* Dragonsong magazine; CAW Australia; Vol 2 No 7 – Autumn 1994

James Woodford of the Sydney Morning Herald; *Unearthed: Australia's lost civilization;* the Age newspaper; 21/9/1996

Come walk the paths that the old ones walk,
come dance the dances they taught us
Come sing the songs that the old ones sang,
for the magick now has caught us

(from 'Woman of the Earth' written by
Adrienne Piggott of Spiral Dance)

www.ingramcontent.com/pod-product-compliance
Lightning Source LLC
Chambersburg PA
CBHW051955290426
44110CB00015B/2255